Calling of God

Kenneth E. Hagin

Chapter 1
'GIFTS DIFFERING....'

For the gifts and calling of God are without repentance.

— Romans 11:29

For as we have many members in one body, and all members have not the same office:

So we, being many, are one body in Christ, and every one members one of another.

Having then gifts differing according to the grace that is given to us....

— Romans 12:4-6

When Paul wrote this letter to the Church at Rome, he didn't divide it into chapters and verses; he just wrote a letter to them. Men in recent times have divided his letters into chapters and verses for the sake of easy reference.

In the twelfth chapter, Paul continues the discussion he began in the eleventh chapter: the gifts and calling of God. You may think as you read the twelfth chapter that he's talking about the gifts of the Holy Spirit referred to in First Corinthians 12, but he isn't.

You see, there are four different Greek words that are translated "gift" or "gifts." You have to understand that to really understand what the Spirit of God is saying here through Paul.

For example, we see the "gift" of eternal life in connection with salvation, and the "gift" of the Holy Spirit. The Greek word used here means "giving as to a pauper," or "a gratuity." Of course, salvation and the baptism of the Holy Spirit are free gifts; you can't merit them.

However, the word "gifts" in our texts, Romans 11:29; 12:4-6, means an "endowment" or "enduement" of the Holy Spirit. Paul's really talking here about ministries or offices — the gifts and calling of God.

People are gifted by the Holy Spirit to stand in certain offices, but we're not all endowed by the Spirit to do the same things, or to stand in the same offices. To put it another way, people are anointed by the Holy Spirit to obey certain callings, but we don't all have the same gift or anointing. We *do* have the same Spirit, but there are degrees and measures of anointing.

We can see from Romans 12:6,7 that Paul is talking about different gifts and ministries.

ROMANS 12:6,7
6 Having then GIFTS differing according to the

grace that is given to us, whether prophecy, let us prophesy according to the proportion of faith;

7 Or ministry, let us wait on our ministering: or he that teacheth, on teaching.

You know as well as I do that everybody is not called to be a teacher in the Body of Christ. Of course, a person could teach another whatever he or she knows — and probably could do a good job. But there's a difference in teaching someone what you know and being really called of God, anointed by the Holy Spirit, and equipped, endowed, and endued by the Spirit of God to stand in the *office* of teacher.

Not everybody is called to be a pastor. Thank God for the pastoral office. We need even more pastors, because their office is needed and necessary. People need an overseer; they need that "shepherd." (The Greek word translated "pastor" is also translated "shepherd," and vice versa.) So thank God for that anointing, that enduement. I don't have it, because that's not my calling.

I know something about the calling or anointing of the teacher, because one of my callings is to be a teacher; the other is to stand in the office of prophet.

One thing I want you to see from our very pertinent, explicit text, Romans 11:29, is that *"the gifts and calling of God are WITHOUT REPENTANCE."* In other words, God is not going to go back on His call on your life — that's it!

I wasn't a part of the early days of the Pentecostal Movement because I was born and raised a Southern Baptist. I received the baptism of the Holy Spirit in 1937, and I came into the Pentecostal Movement the following year, after receiving "the left foot of fellowship" from among the Baptists.

I have learned about the early days of the Pentecostal Movement by talking to people who were there. Once while attending a monthly fellowship meeting down in East Texas, I met an older gentleman who was visiting from California. He was a minister of that Full Gospel denomination.

While we were having dinner on the grounds, he and another minister, one of the main speakers, told how they had received the baptism with the Holy Spirit back at the turn of the century.

Some people there in Texas did receive the baptism of the Holy Spirit at that time. In fact, Brother W. J. Seymour went from Alvin, Texas, below Houston, to California in 1906 and was mightily used in the outpouring of the Holy Spirit in the old Azusa Street Mission in Los Angeles.

As they talked, these men said that in the early days of the Pentecostal Movement, nearly all of them preached on Hebrews 6 and 10, telling people that if they ever fell away (backslid), it would be impossible for them to get back into fellowship with God. The devil used such teaching to rob, blind, and destroy God's people because of their ignorance of the Word.

Let's look at these verses, because they fit into our discussion about the gifts and calling of God.

HEBREWS 6:4-6

4 For it is impossible for those who were once enlightened, and have tasted of the heavenly gift, and were made partakers of the Holy Ghost,
5 And have tasted the good word of God, and the powers of the world to come,
6 If they shall fall away, to renew them again unto repentance; seeing they crucify to themselves the Son of God afresh, and put him to an open shame.

HEBREWS 10:26-29

26 For if we sin wilfully after that we have received the knowledge of the truth, there remaineth no more sacrifice for sins,
27 But a certain fearful looking for of judgment and fiery indignation, which shall devour the adversaries.
28 He that despised Moses' law died without mercy under two or three witnesses:
29 Of how much sorer punishment, suppose ye, shall

he be thought worthy, who hath trodden under foot the Son of God, and hath counted the blood of the covenant, wherewith he was sanctified, an unholy thing, and hath done despite unto the Spirit of grace?

One of these older preachers then told how he had held a street meeting one Saturday afternoon down in Corsicana, Texas.

He didn't take up an offering, but God so blessed the people that they threw money at his feet. Now, this was at the turn of the century, when money wasn't plentiful like it is now, but he got a nice offering. When he counted it afterwards, he had $28. He felt rich. That was a whole month's salary for that time.

After his meeting, the preacher was walking along the boardwalk — their sidewalks were made out of boards then — and an old drunk he knew from other street meetings came crashing out of the swinging doors of one of the saloons. (They had open saloons in Texas in those days.)

The old drunk staggered up to the preacher, got nose to nose with him, and demanded, "Say 'hallelujah'!" Then he backed off and repeated his demand: "You say 'hallelujah' or I'm going to knock you down!"

The preacher related, "I was stupid enough to say 'hallelujah,' and he hit me."

The drunk knocked the preacher through the window of the saloon, and that's the last thing he remembered. He fell into a pile of beer bottles, and spectators said that when he got up, he had a beer bottle in each hand and nearly beat the old drunk to death.

He told us, "I was so mad, that I can't remember any of it."

When he came to himself, the spectators were pulling him off the drunk. The police arrested both of them, and the preacher had to pay a fine for fighting — a Pentecostal, Full Gospel, tongue-talking preacher fighting!

Now, according to what he'd heard taught, once you've sinned like this and backslid, you can't get back to God. So he thought, *When I die, I'm going to go to hell, so I might as well get all I can out of this life.*

With the few dollars he had left, he caught a train, went to Houston, and lived it up. He finally wound up out in California. He was away from God for about 12 years, drinking, gambling, running around with women, and everything else. But he said the Holy Spirit kept dealing with him.

There weren't many Full Gospel churches out in California then, but he looked in the telephone directory and found a church of his own denomination. He called the pastor and said, "I want to come and talk to you." The pastor said, "All right."

He told the pastor, "If I've sinned away my day of grace and I can't get back in, I wish the Holy Ghost would leave me alone."

This pastor said, "Oh, well, we saw we were wrong in teaching that — that's not right." He prayed with the fellow and he got back into fellowship with God. And the minute he did, "the preach" was still there — because *the gifts and calling of God are without repentance.*

He had left his wife and several children back in Texas. The first thing he did was to get on the telephone and try to locate them. (He hadn't contacted them before, because he thought he was hell-bound.)

He was reunited with his family in California and he began to preach again. He became a leader in his Full Gospel denomination! He was mightily anointed and used of God. When I came into the Pentecostal Movement I heard of him. I was told that the anointing on him was greater than on most preachers — because the gifts and calling of God are without repentance.

It's to be regretted that he lost his temper and sinned. He wouldn't have if he'd known more about the Bible. It says in Hosea 4:6 that the people of God are destroyed *"for the lack of knowledge."* The Bible teaches, *"Be ye angry, and sin not . . ."* (Eph. 4:26).

Let's examine Hebrews 10:29 again. Notice what the unpardonable or unforgiveable sin actually is: "*. . .who hath trodden under foot the Son of God, and hath counted the blood of the covenant, wherewith he was sanctified, an unholy thing. . . .*" Counting the blood of Jesus an unholy thing is the sin referred to in these Scriptures.

In church circles, theologians as a whole are not too sure just who wrote Hebrews. It sounds like Paul's writings to me, and one time when Jesus appeared to me in a vision, I asked Him, and He told me that Paul wrote it. And I believe he did!

Paul is writing here to Hebrew Christians. If you know anything about church history, you know that when these Jews accepted Christ, they were excommunicated from their family and their fellow Jews. They had it pretty hard, and some of them were tempted to go back to their old life in Judaism. They could have had it easier; their friends and family would have stood with them; and they would have been helped financially and materially. But, you see, if they had done that, then they would have been counting the blood they were sanctified with an unholy thing.

In other words, they would have been saying that Jesus is not the Son of God — Jesus is not the Messiah — He is just a man. If He is just a man, His blood is unholy. But if He's the divine Son of God — if He's the Messiah — His blood is not unholy; His blood is holy! And that was the sin Paul was writing about.

Did that young preacher commit such a sin? Granted, he lost his temper and came up off the floor beating the drunk over the head with beer bottles, but that's not "trodding under foot the Son of God"! That's not the unpardonable sin. He did not count the blood of Jesus an unholy thing. He did not deny that Jesus Christ is the Divine Son of God.

The devil has used wrong teaching from this passage of Scripture to hinder a lot of people. Don't let him hinder you.

God doesn't repent. The Greek word translated "repentance" means a change of mind, a change of purpose, a change of will. God never changes, so He doesn't change His will; He doesn't change His purpose; and He doesn't change His mind. Hallelujah! The gifts and calling of God are without repentance.

God had *called* this man; God had *gifted* this man; and God didn't change His mind even though the man sinned and failed. The minute he got back into fellowship with God, the call was still there. What should he do with it? Thank God, he obeyed God and became a nationally known minister.

Chapter 2
'I A PEACHER'

Whatever God called you to do — whatever He gifted you to do — whatever He endowed and endued you by the Spirit of God to do — the call is still there. The endowment is still there. The enduement is still there. If you'll *obey* it and walk with God, often the anointing will be *increased*.

However, just because we're called to the ministry doesn't mean we're all called to do the same thing. One place where ministers often miss it is in trying to be a "jack of all trades and a master of none" in the ministry.

Even when I was a young minister, I heard other ministers say of certain church programs, "We all ought to be doing that." No, if God didn't call and equip you to do it, you shouldn't be doing it.

That would be like saying, "We all ought to be pastors." I tried to be a pastor for 12 years, and I was out of the will of God. I didn't know I was out of the will of God, and God permitted it for a while, but the time came when He said, "You're going to have to do something else — or else!" And I said, "Well, I believe I will."

Being only in the permissive will of God is like washing your feet with your socks on. You may not realize what's wrong, but you know something isn't quite right; something just doesn't feel right.

So I know that everybody shouldn't be a pastor, although I tell our Rhema students that I think every evangelist ought to be made to pastor for at least two years. It would do him good. He'd learn how to cooperate with the pastor. He'd learn *not* to say certain things.

And then every pastor ought to be forced out into field ministry for a minimum of two years, and he'd learn something too. We need one another. We need different ministries.

In Romans 12:4, Paul said "*. . .we have many members in one body, and all members have not the same office.*" Paul is using the physical body as a type of the Body of Christ.

In verse 5, he writes, "*So we, being many, are one body in Christ, and every one members one of another.*" Whether you like it or not, if people are really born again, they're members of the same Body you are. That's absolutely the truth. And you have to be very careful how you behave toward fellow believers. Be sure you walk in love toward them if you want to stay out of trouble. You can open the door for the devil and get into all kinds of trouble if you don't walk in love.*

Paul said we are "*one body in Christ.*" Christ doesn't have two bodies; He's not twins. There's one Body, and everyone is a member "*one of another.*"

The Body of Christ as a whole is in disarray today because we don't recognize one another as we ought to. We don't realize that we are members one of another even though we have *"gifts differing according to the grace that is given to us . . ."* (v. 6).

If we're not careful, we'll try to do everything everybody else is doing. Let's do only what God has called us to do; then we'll become more expert at it.

I feel sorry for these people. Even some of our Rhema students stumble around, wondering whether they're called or not. Rhema Bible Training Center is designed to train people for the ministry, but everybody doesn't go into full-time ministry. For example, some are in the ministry of helps.

Our text talks about two things: "gifts and calling." Am I called or not? What am I called to do? We're members of one another — we're all members of the same Body — but what is our place in the Body? What is our calling?

We're all called to salvation, isn't that right? We're called to be saved and filled with the Holy Spirit. And everybody in a sense is called to be a preacher, because to preach means "to proclaim" or "to tell," and everybody ought to be a witness for Jesus.

But there are specific ministries: apostle, prophet, evangelist, pastor, and teacher. Are you called, or not?

I've never been bothered with that question. I don't know how to relate to people who don't know whether or not they're called to preach. The thought *You're not called* never once occurred to me in my entire life. Never! I've never had a shadow of a doubt about it.

I've just known all of my life — even as a little, bitty kid — that I was going to be a preacher. I knew it in my spirit. (People need to examine their spirits. The trouble is, they examine their heads, and there's not much there!)

People would ask my older brother, "What are you going to be when you grow up?" We were born and raised in Texas, so he'd always say he was going to be a cowboy or a truck driver. They wouldn't ask me — they thought I was too young to know — but my relatives said I would always speak up, even though I couldn't talk plainly yet, "I a peacher!"

Grandpa always had a garden out behind the house. After I got to be 3 to 5 years of age, I'd go out in the garden and preach to the cabbage heads. (If we didn't eat the cabbage when it was fresh, Granny would make sauerkraut out of it, can it, and use it in many different ways.) I tell people I sometimes think I'm still preaching to cabbage heads! Those cabbage heads never changed their expression; there was never any response.

When I got tired of preaching to cabbage heads, I'd go over and preach to the bean vines for a while. Then, in the winter time, when we didn't have any garden, I'd go to the barn, climb up in the hayloft, and preach to the bales of hay.

You say, "What did you preach?"

I don't know. I just had that "preach" in me. If you've got it in you, it's going to come out.

You don't have to train a rooster to crow! I could stand up on a fence and "crow," but I'd have to put it on. But it's automatic for the rooster.

I did all right as long as I was a little child. I knew all along what I wanted to be. As I got older, I could answer people when they asked, "What are you going to be when you grow up?" I'd say, "A preacher — that's what I'm going to be!"

---

*For more information on this subject, see Rev. Kenneth E. Hagin's minibooks *How To Walk in Love* and *Love Never Fails.*

Chapter 3
THE AGE OF ACCOUNTABILITY

After I reached the age of accountability, when people asked me what I was going to be when I grew up, I'd reply, "I'm going to be a lawyer."

I'd go listen to lawyers argue cases all day long at the courthouse. I'd sit up in the balcony. And I was sure, when I was 11 or 12, that I could have done better than some of those lawyers, because I'd heard so many cases argued. I don't know whether I could have or not, but that was my thinking.

We saw that Paul said, "I was alive without the law once." He meant his spirit was alive to God. Where does the human spirit come from, anyway? The Bible says in Hebrews 12:9 that God is "the Father of spirits."

Only people who are born again go to heaven, it is said. What about little babies who have died? They never were born again. Where do they go?

My mother was the oldest child in her family. There was a boy several years younger than she who died when he was barely 9.

Her family lived out in the country then — this was before 1900. Grandpa Drake had a country store and later a farm. There were no churches out there. Finally Grandpa and some of the neighbors got together and started a Sunday School on Sunday afternoons in the school building. They got a preacher to agree to come out and preach once a month and finally twice a month.

Little Ernest never was baptized in water and never made any kind of a profession of faith. The year Ernest died, Grandpa had planted cotton right up to one side of the house. Grandpa's store, an old-fashioned country store, was on the other side of the house. One Saturday

Grandpa closed up at noon time as always. Granny had the noon meal on the table and they were all sitting there eating. Momma was 11 years old and Ernest was barely 9.

Granny looked out the window at the cotton and said, "Well, Ernest, you're going to get your heart's desire. We're going to start picking cotton Monday morning."

He replied, "No, not me, Momma."

He was always such a good boy — so obedient — and for him to say "No, not me," surprised them.

"Why, Honey," she said, "what makes you say that?"

He said, "I'm going to be up there with Jesus," and he pointed heavenward.

They wondered what he meant. But when Monday came, he was up in heaven with Jesus.

It always bothered Granny that Ernest had never made any kind of profession of faith. She worried about his salvation, because the church she went to taught that you aren't saved unless you are baptized in water a certain way, and he'd never been baptized in water.

But his spirit was still alive to God, because he knew when he was going home. Where do you think he went? He told them beforehand where he was going; his spirit was alive to God.

Sooner or later, a child reaches the age of accountability. Usually it's anywhere from age 9 to 12. It may be younger with some. It's according to their intellect, environment, and influence — their upbringing.

Paul says something very interesting about this in Romans 7:9, *"For I was alive without the law once...."* He couldn't be talking about being *physically* alive, because he was physically alive afterwards. What is he talking about, then? He is talking about being *spiritually* alive "without the law once."

The verse continues, *"...but when the commandment came, sin revived, and I died."* When the commandment came, he didn't die physically, because he was still alive as he was writing to them.

What's he talking about, then? Paul is saying that without the law, he was alive to God. But when the commandment came — *when he reached the age of accountability and knew the difference between right and wrong* — sin revived. What does he mean, sin revived? That sin nature (original sin, some call it) was there all the time in his flesh. It revived and he died spiritually; that is, he lost his spiritual life.

I know exactly when this happened to me. I was 9 years of age. The commandment came, sin revived, and I "died." Did I cease to exist? Certainly not!

This is where people get so confused with terminology; particularly with the phrase "spiritual death." When they hear this phrase, they interpret it to mean *physical* death, but that's not what it means.

Paul doesn't mean he ceased to exist. What did he mean? He meant his spirit was not alive to God anymore. And my spirit wasn't alive to God from age 9 until I got saved at age 15.

The minute I was born again, my spirit was alive to God again, and that call was right there. I didn't know what the call was, other than a call to preach. In fact, the first thing I said to God after I was born again was, "You get me up from here, and I'll go preach."

I was bedfast 16 months before I was healed, but, thank God, I was healed. I left that bed preaching, and I've been preaching ever since. I celebrated 50 years in the ministry in August 1984.

Chapter 4
A VOICE FROM HEAVEN

The gifts and calling of God are without repentance.

I preached wherever the door opened. I was just a 17-year-old boy. I went to high school, taught a Sunday School class, and spoke to young people's groups. There weren't any Full Gospel churches in our town yet, but I had been healed, so I would tell people about healing, and I'd lay hands on them and get them healed.

I'd go visit some church, and if they wanted somebody to mow the yard, I was the first one to volunteer. If they wanted someone to sweep the floor, I was the first one to volunteer. (When you volunteer to work for God, He's liable to promote you!)

I would also lead home prayer meetings. We'd have a Bible study and do some praying, but not a lot, because we all prayed silently.

Then I started pastoring a country church when I was 18 (I turned 19 the next Sunday). I pastored various churches over the next 12 years, and then God led me into the field ministry.

Eventually I became discouraged and left the field, feeling it was too difficult being away from my family. I was about to take another pastorate when the Lord dealt with me.

I heard a voice speak to me from heaven. To me it was audible. And it was just as real as any man's voice I've ever heard. It was a man's voice. I know it must have been Jesus.

He said, "I want you to go teach my people faith. I have taught you faith through my Word. I have permitted you to go through certain experiences, and you learned faith. You learned faith through my Word and by experiences. Now go teach my people what I've taught you. Go teach my people faith!"

I teach on many other things, yet faith is one subject I've stayed with faithfully. I'm not disobedient to what God said. I've done what God said to do. I've taught faith, and I was out there when no one else was.

I've been called everything in the world except something good, but I've just smiled. Bless their hearts — some people don't understand.

When I stand before the Lord, I want to be able to say, "I was not disobedient to what You said."

Whatever God has called you to do — whatever He's gifted and endued you by the Holy Spirit to accomplish — He hasn't changed His mind about it. One day you will have to give an account of what you did with that calling. Obedience to God's call will bring blessing and satisfaction to your life.

If you're a Christian and have been sensing that something isn't quite right in your life, perhaps you need to look down inside your spirit and ask yourself, "Am I doing what God has called me to do?"

If God has called you to do a specific work for Him and you've not been doing it, that calling isn't going to go away. The best thing you can do is to step out and obey God.

I've never regretted one day of following the Lord. The joy and blessings I've known have more than made up for any hardships I've encountered along the way. God said in His Word, "*If ye be willing and obedient, ye shall eat the good of the land*" (Isa. 1:19). I'm glad I obeyed God!

If you'll simply step out and do what He's called you to do — whether it's to proclaim His Word, or to assist others through the ministry of helps — you'll find yourself walking into the blessings of God and a greater fulfillment in your life than you ever dreamed possible.